Psalms at the Present Time

Psalms at the Present Time

Darryl Lorenzo Wellington

Flowstone Press

Psalms at the Present Time

Copyright © 2021 Darryl Lorenzo Wellington

Cover Image © Marya Kirby. Used with permission.

First Flowstone Press Edition • November 2021
ISBN 978-1-945824-50-0

Flowstone Press,
an Imprint of Left Fork
www.leftforkbooks.com

God is a front porch dweller

Table of Contents

God and Death 3

Poetry Dedicated to Strangers, Lives and Others 4
  in Starry Disbelief

Lamp-Lit 6

Notebook Time is Any Time at 6 AM … 7

A Standard Rhyming Dictionary 8

Devil Plays Mean Cards 9

Narcissistic Father To his Family Tree 10

A Pretense 11

A Plant Named *les Liaisons Dangereuses* 12
  Rises from the Watery Depths

Racing Thoughts on Gentrification 13

Psalm Sequence
  Psalm I: Peace of Mind 15
  Psalm II: The Remembered Past 17
  Psalm III: Dwellings 19
  Psalm IV: Dark at the Fresh Start 20
  Psalm V: Come and Join the Dark 22
  Psalm VI 23

The Next Psalm 24

The Summer Cycle 25

Snow Blanketing the Hills, at the Eastern Prospect, ... 26
  past the Family House

A Fantastic World 27

A Mad Carousel Poem 28

The Shriveled Condom 35

Autumnal 40

The Room Light 41

Downtown Lounge   42
And They Say   43
November Beginnings   46
Fragmented by Frenetic Erasure   48
Pantoums for James Meredith   52
How to Live with Racism, In Times Like These   54
And that Same Old Song and Savage Splendor   56
Stranger in a Legal Land   59
A Southern Plantation Memory   60
The Man Staring into the Partial Dark: A Ghazal   61
Sunlight Erasing Lines, Margins on a Pencil Drawing   62
A Spiritual Emanation/ Ejaculation   63
Easy Street. Or, The Year of Getting a Driver's License   64
    and Exciting Eldritch Regions of Consciousness
Nature Proem   66
Days of Protest   67
Contemplating Homelessness   71

Acknowledgments   75
About the Author   77

Psalms at the Present Time

God and Death

God is a front porch dweller. God is a long-time neighbor who you used to imagine could become a closer friend — someone that you have become accustomed to judging at a distance.

***

Death is a beautiful woman, infamous, inviolable, sans emotional attachments. She is too beautiful for human emotions. No one remains surprised anymore. No one doubts her majestic impersonality. Strange, then, because tears, cries, and hysterical lamentations accompany her arrival.

***

Death advises. Please marry, or fall in love, or make love in fantasy to shadows lacking corporeal substance. This will lessen the disappointment, the final loss, the bitterness, at the end.

***

Be wary. Stranger.

Life, the felicitous wife; Death, the less kind, less forgiving mistress.

Love yourself less openly. If you love your wife too passionately, too intensely, too proudly, Death, the cryptic, closeted mistress, becomes jealous.

***

Death strews advice like funeral flowers.

Poetry Dedicated to Strangers, Lives and Others
in Starry Disbelief

A new self at rebirthing
inarticulate and stupid
is a gangly doll
half plastic, half human.
The universe slopes
such an undeclamatory evening
like a tilted glass
the stars gone milky
the stars gone whitish milky
near shadowless absence
the grass the color of
porous-hearted nostalgia the color of
a still life reminiscence the still life the color of
Goldenlight crackers, milk, and honey.

***

The grief is implicit
inside the sharing of stories
Do you mean the sharing of stones?
regardless whether I ask
slowly, methodically, like a toy simulacrum.
too much like a metronome,
the chess pieces measuring an end game,
the small pawns marching toward an upheaval
the upheaval weightier than a cathedral
Do you mean weightier than a culmination?
so that I speak beneath a cathedral tomb
and I ask whether I myself am duplicitous
a toy inside an echolalic simulacrum

Do I mean the grief is implicit?
while others speak spastically,
helplessly, babbling several voices,
while others break into tears
while others withhold so much judgment
insensibly to themselves/ against the world/
and from the world against themselves
their hard luck cases plunk like stones
pelting the cathedral moat waters.
Do I mean to share the stones with the dreary waters?

Lamp-Lit

The moth casts a giant presence,
        — why call its shadow an absence?
formlessness,
loneliness,
like a pockmarked
hole widening an opening
into space, time, space, place,
of course, and time's eclipse
implied by the shape

that's flung
against a wall. This desert island-like *en masse* blear —
like an ink stain against the wall's calligraphy.
Accept that this is not an absence
Accept that this is a presence
Accept that the lividly solitary presence
may change moment to moment
indefinitely left behind by light's absence.

Notebook Time is Any Time at 6 AM ...

risen crude early
hyperactively mindful
parched sun: riven laughter
Scenes pictured indistinctly —
poor vision adjusts

morn astigmatic
marriage of thought and action
slowly unravels
her journals reflect
time's stately unconsciousness

A Standard Rhyming Dictionary

        proffers the interesting
and never-ending possibility
that an irredeemably solitary *emptiness*
can be meaningfully relieved via *cunnilingus*
flipping random *pages* past the *ages*
and all roads lead to love
and lustiness
which is rhyme. There are no words
like syrupy assonances
like music hall reverberations
nor haunted echo chamber effects
for where we are
going. The loneliness between us,
and manifold mystery, too, is speechless.
The best guidebook is *sweet* and *effete*.
A pair of self-entwined
and artful tongues
set us on this
silently chiming and wordlessly rhyming
wayward path, dumbstruck,
hopelessly
idealistic back then and still unknowing.

Devil Plays Mean Cards

The Devil lays down a suite of smoking jackets.
His bitten, ashen fingernails a deathly affront.
He easily recalls the King, Queen, and Jack by first name
knowing the royal crescents have relied on him.
A table rattles. A sweet suite crackles. Like a singing lash.
His winning hand is an assemblage familiar.

Narcissistic Father To his Family Tree

A Christmas ditty after Sir Walter Raleigh

Three things there be challenging my faith — and patience —
Around the table, until we grow asunder far.
His Word Made Flesh, they meet in all one place
And when they meet, they one another mar;
And they be these: the cough, the sneeze, the sob,
A grainy cough spreads righteous fear contagion.
This snot unholiness: please cover the turkey pot.
The sob, my family tree, betokeneth self-annihilation.
Mark well, family, while these assemble not
Christ is in the oven; the spirit is flesh; the wine breathes;
Until a sneeze, a sob (child?) and all four table legs rot.
Rife corruption at the placemat threatens the many
Clumsy generations. A stalwart family tree bent bacterial.
Ah, Christmas, when the disinherited learn *hell is immaterial.*

A Pretense

down the corridor

Two dancers, of a peculiar pair,
  One hops toward the other,
    Leg raised,
   strung back.
One handicapped. Imagine hinds crudely tied together.
Two dancers, of a peculiar pair

The other waits immobile to accept
      A crippled spirit, a bowlegged
          -ly limping dog
             a pitiful thing so kneeless,
a beast that has no spent force left
lingering. Imagine: near certain blood death midwinter.

The facility is kept private, silent,
secreted from sprawl. Unopened to guests.
A white shirted man, however, has set out chairs.
The dancers' knobby ankles *creak, creak* on the floor mat
conjuring the woods surround. Imagine: squirrels, mice, small
birds rasping inside the walls.

An audience attends

A special group attends by pre-requested
      preordained commitment to
         a signatured agreement.
  We will not display many emotions.
     We understand the pretense
concurrent to rules: no coughs; no shuffles. None.
      X'd: suspicious sighs, grins, chortles, tears.

    Please.

    No applause.

A Plant Named *les Liaisons Dangereuses*
Rises from the Watery Depths

                   rising
like a razorblade's threat,
like a reaper's scythe
drawing from the surf
the loneliest, lightest backlash,
stitching, unstitching, leaving beach
shadows purpler than remnant shore
-light stunned in crimson swathes
blood-colored, or infected itself
— at the hour the moonlight's
a suicide haunted by its tidal victim.

Racing Thoughts on Gentrification

in Charleston, South Carolina

If you can imagine
all the *haute couture/ storefronts/*
bulging at the seams/
beware the waistline
a suit that can't fit on a Goliathan
nor inhibit his effortless largesse/
Sunday morning crowds besting
Saturday night fevers
strolling into the pithiest *bon mots*
custom painted signs
challenging man's idiomatic inventory
a storefront Renaissance
then you can/ painfully/
reimagine in
-glorious Black Sundays
innumerable vacancies
ratcheting up no such sales
inside gritty metal cups
that can't rattle. Downtown's
failed reclamation project.
Charleston's afterthought.
Blighted blocks universalized.
Memory's emotional drought.
No taste. Touch. Tang.
No streetwise purview. Seeds. Spawn.
No *Maxine's Restaurant* church coven.
And divine
from the left unsaid, flickering
socially acceptable memories on, flicking

sentimental neighborhood tall tales on
then off, polarities puzzled, like a light switch.
The sentiments in between
sketching a picturesque light and dark

make a parable. Though no one
inside the centerpiece paradigm
one city/ one coastline/
where the moral is given
and the temperature is taken
will say who is responsible —
nor how the visions possibly
describe one lowcountry/
one love/
one pulse beat wandering the peninsula amicably.

Psalm I: Peace of Mind

— home,
go back.
There will be people home
and they will be alive
with salutations among the living,
bristling sex, energy, body and spirit,
and the cries that trail behind all that jazz.
There were people in your dreams
last night
and while who can say if they're bygone
neither were they living.
That will be the difference
between places of peace and welcoming
and a place of the skulls.
Places of peace. And ruin. And the only difference.

***

Peace of mind will scurry, like fire ants scattering,
a flight of frightened and submissive flags,
a Northbound/ Southbound/ shirking and directionless migration.

Peace of mind bustles, a disintegrating hive,
hording, blazoning in between savage confusion and total organization.

Peace of mind scavenges the tinsel that never replenishes.
The magpie's children starve, or grow into stubborn spirits.

Peace of mind will take a long while to cultivate
and an abacus of days to convince
yourself in spite of yourself/ the untimely
pulse beat that dissents/ you aren't
nostalgizing its green meadows into birth and beatitude

patience of ants/ nitpicking/
rebuilding/ blanched
to yellow nothingness
beneath the summer
wash/ sleep blessed underneath the intensity
and swirl
and cleanliness rinsing
skulls and bones/ places of peace to phantasm
and ruin/ the longest hours to the shortest to lose

Psalm II: The Remembered Past

and the finest
hours that you
have enjoyed this year
come with strings attached,
like frills hanging from kites.

The remembered past
is windlessly unwinding; the present
is a castle of stone
slowly sinking
giving sway

O kings O kingdoms
suffering tidal lashes
nibbling at the edges
of Camelot: the castle
in memory still Caliban's retreat

bedeviled tropical island fruit
Camelot island has been
losing peripheral ground
to the watercourses
nobody remembers
the rumors anymore

back in the day, the old school
and scatology, the stories
before the seventh grade
surrounding the island lighthouse
in that not-so-distant
past prefiguring the

present period's
apropos of nothing much
before the nostalgic erosion
dissolves Camelot and Chronos
and all that's essential that is left
like an aspirin in water.

Psalm III: Dwellings

She *thoughtlessly* thought she married a man, not a single digit, just like any other man, not a finger always pointed in accusation. Home. History. Dice. Cards. A broom. A broomstick. A mop. A rag. A wet rag. A duster. A scrub brush. A scrub brush holder. A nail in a wall. A wall without tears. A sink with a running nose. A sink with a kidney infection. A sink with cramps. A sink with dishpan hands. A stone bird. A stone bird from K-Mart. A migrant flock. A tea plate. Hung on the wall. An illustrated plate. The image of the Last Supper. This bread is my body. A photograph. A man with full cheeks. A man choking on his food. His mouth hung open. His hand covering it up. His manners impeccable. A *faux* preacher. A glass top table. A glass top table filled with photographs. A Cross. A dangling icon. A pretty bauble. A prayer of the day. An illustrated calendar. On the calendar, one day has been scratched out: far in the future — not only checked, x'd out — that day will not exist, when it comes, it will not *happen*. The day she deceives her husband, her hand and mind fantastically coordinated. She picks up the phone, and her gesture throws a shadow of her hand clutching a teethed comb. An iron skillet. A sharpened file. A weapon. Using it, though her thoughts jar, she calls the number — preserved under the bowl where her dentures lay in frothy water — of a Realtor who can market value *her history*. Breath sucking through her gums, as she does when she is fitfully asleep — though she isn't asleep, though she is living a day that is outside her chronological years — her chronological life span — she calls with a wrinkled hand and, with a shadowy weapon, with an angry pencil, writes it down.

Psalm IV: Dark at the Fresh Start

Dark that lasts so long
wafts like a fanning plant, so lullaby
-like. And spreads. And sways.
And thins. And thins. And bends.
Remember, however:
Dark never breaks

like a treetop bough.
Dark is a means to an end.
The creepy crawlers ubiquitously
unshutter their eyes
tonight, less
to gather the world
to see anything at all
than weigh the blight.
The blight in general
wafts like a fanning plant,
they know this.
They study the gradations
like living situations:
Nothing much is lost.
It lightens at the edges

like sleep.
Not a modicum wasted in dissipation,
in night-speak marginalia; the green
-species crawlers whether they
pigeonhole the archness
suck up or see-through
the nocturnal mulch
lay the wet sounds in ground in storage.
Dark that lasts so long.
White noise. It bulges in their purses.

***

Remember, however
like a hyped gangly child,
dark will skip, leap, scamper,
slipping through the thickest heavyset bushes,
outrace you to the margin-line,
the flowing water's edge,
beats you, sucker, beats you down

Psalm V: Come and Join the Dark

Come join the family darks
who graduated the public schools, skulls dilated
larger than exotic house plants. So
far everything in life has grown from
seed and watering. There has been bitterness, too,
in the night, nights of too many
stark tears, the darkness a peculiar
skittering, skittering in the ceiling —

shy as a vanishing fawn; dark the fabled tree
where the stillborn baby lies buried
dark inside a shoebox somewhere back
that you have heard rumored since
the family get together where Uncle Lee
drank so much he took a pee
and out of his piss sprang the first flowers of spring.
But if someone who was nobody's brother or
sister's favorite foolish foil sisterly meddled
in the middle of a fabulous story, gro-
tesque inbreeding, stolen kisses beneath
flowering trees, incestuous activities in the hay,
shit, mush, pig crust barely hidden in the straw,
a mouth twisted in disgust like a backwards cap,
he would be handed a gravedigger's shovel
unwashed from a throwaway pile and pointed
in very dark directions; he would be told
— *sorry*, they whispered, snickered, gestured, *see* —
to do a job that was too dark for you or me.

Psalm VI

You don't fall asleep in any one place.
You shunt several places, states, saturnalia
and balance them. And walk suspension bridges
no less than the mischievous showcase seals
chasing the bright red rubber balls, chancily spinning.
Several cityscapes, lines. The way the worst of it
breaks inside you along
-side the best of it. The final judgment
is no less random than critiquing a hotel room
in an Arctic zone.
Whether this was *good sleep, bad sleep,*
good sleep, bad sleep: too many factors
in increments readjust the room temperature to the body.

The Next Psalm

— bellies pallid/ swimmingly transparent/
fishy-mouthed
a wormy, intractable iridescence
less phlegmatic than filmy
as piquant as caviar eggs/ a sudden gloaming/
at shore side
soulless all under
crawling like slugs
near the rocks sullen.
Running in schools
flecked silvery —
and harvested beneath bone whitish
sheds, semi-precious,
elemental,
more perfect than stone
richly polished
washed of celestial excess
man's space age aquatic —
Our palms
blanched
colorless as asteroids
craggily knuckled
and witless.
We set them aside.
We lay them down.
We lay them
ceremonially down: our Bibles,
the sodden bulk bulging, spreading
lachrymosely wet sheets, wet, slick papyri,
then lifted our hands.

The Summer Cycle

I have no dog in
any fight with summer flowers
thirsty in autumn

grasping for breath. The sultry
summer invariably
lets go its fire. Fire —

for some plants —
is mere transition
a sudden unraveling

during a breezy life cycle.
How they thrive
like summer children

intuiting death
is the strangest
moment of activity

— a hormonal rush
that you can't survive.
And they survive

— like the melancholy *lieder* still survives.

Song cycles of *fleurs* and childhood deaths

seasonally counterbalancing growth.

June fires flaking paths of blinding
stormwater crushing wreckage
then the dreamless school days after.

Snow Blanketing the Hills, at the Eastern Prospect, past the Family House

Come see. From the balcony.
The frosty tips
The iron peaks.
The short reliefs. The silvery white
hairs combed by sunlight.
If you shudder, cough, cough,
wheeze, moments later you'll sigh. Then.
Tell me. Is sister sleeping?
Is the landscape weeping?
Is Abigail peeking? This landscape
so stiflingly bleak and echolalic —
Is a white carpet worth a wintry
hemisphere?
— frost's babbling brook
but mutely monochromatic
silently
or stealthily apocalyptic.
Come look at the view — nearer — nearer — nearest —
Nearer the pith.
Snow blanketing the thankless hills.
And you suddenly come to believe
beyond shivering, or comeliness sheer weariness pervades
and the Eastern prospect could be
                              maybe
                should be
    such languor   what sleep itself   is like.

A Fantastic World

Ah. And then he inserted fingers, working his potter's green thumb
Beneath his belt buckle, his salaciously soiled — sardonically sheepish —
Coy planter's hand. And groped his private regions under the school
Desk. A loose button snaps. Pops. Soundless. Seventh grade hopes that sigh
Effortlessly. But he remained attuned to unremarkable *pings*, *plinks*, funny,
Fastidious, amplifying fantastical worlds. His pathetic amour, meanwhile, Ms.
Garvin used a walking stick that *tapped, tapped, tapped*, her fluttering skirts
Harboring secrets that rustled halfway open, blouses, hems, *fleurs*,
Incrementally unloosened. O Ms. Garvin wielded her cane's persistent
Jerkily deathly rhythms. Her spastic steps. Her funereal *shtick*. Rumored
Knells presaged Ms. Garvin's replacement. A forty three year old schoolmarm's
Last days should be lauded with lunchbox apples. Her vivacity regardless,
Muscular Dystrophy, or an unpronounceable motor ailment whose
Nomenclature resisted him stiffened her middle-aged bones. *Here, Ms. Garvin!*
Or. Receive my last gifts, he fantasizes, but other voices assert, she's ill,
Proving neither the rumors valid. Nor his fantastical days inconceivable.
Question: *Why is this particular spring the providence of sex and death?*
Response: Seventh Grade. Seeds burgeoned inseparably from scythed roses.
Scattered thoughts in class. Dragged him toward nature. The playgrounds.
Terrific seasonal parades of tart colors, odors and sweet grasses
Unhinged customary assignments. His handwriting spirals, spinning chaos.
Verily a symbolic history of the fine arts, formal, then free expression, like pre-
World War One Edwardian aesthetics collapsing to ahistorical chaos, striking
X's over his feverish sketches, doodles, curlicues, while his left hand
Yearned that nothing, nothing stymie completion. Every rakish ABC sweated.
Zephyr winds brushed his thighs. Ms. Garvin's cane tapped lightning. And then the spring
                                                                    rains.

A Mad Carousel Poem

The juxtaposition of passages taken from the *King James* Bible — stories, verses and imagery inside pages flipped back and forth at random — the extemporaneous Word draws me to the thin line where my past ends, and ceremony, or selfhood begins.

***

I studied *King James* back then, a little boy becoming a 'bigger' lil' boy raised in Southern Baptist households. My singular experience with the Good Book since/ *since then* meaning since regions of childhood trauma/ pastness/ meaning since *my drama of language and masks*/ happened decades later when I played a sort of psychological game.

***

Precious Lord. Gentle words on the lightest pages. My generation received instructions for the *purpose of rote memorization.* We were frightened to touch our Bibles. We waited to open them, when told. Touch itself insinuated a holy hush — penitent fingers hesitantly folding the pages, sort of *in apologia.*
— back then *I would have been frightened to cavalierly flip through the gold-leafed pages at random*; back then, I *believed the pages were precious*; I believed *the Bible pages were lightweight so that the words lay lightly on the tongue*; I memorized, *For whoever slaps you on the right cheek, turn to him your left cheek. If anyone wants to sue you, and take away your tunic, let him have your cloak also. And whoever compels you to go with him one mile, go with him two.*
Every lesson steered us toward Easter Sunday pageants/ Christmas Eve showcases/ when students recited Gospels. Rote. Recitation. Regurgitation. I could have defended the belief that the Bible was "a talking book" because I never saw anybody cracking it open without beginning to babble. My only memorable experience with the Good Book since then/ *since then* meaning since the historical era of lip, learning and tongue/ it occurred the night I played with self, guilt, serendipity and memory irresponsibly. *Since then* meaning since I should have learned better/ lots better. I suckered myself.

***

The *King James* swirled on an imaginary pedestal. Back then/ I never completed homework assignments, nor opened my *King James* in my room at home because it felt too insidious for it to occupy the same space alongside my 13 years old interests, comic books, soft porn novels, swarthy sneakers, dirt, grit, snot, slept-on sheets, socks, semen, and pubescent smells, and the way to protect this holiness must be to let it be undisturbed — absent a distinguished golden lectern. I couldn't bring myself to answer *What is the meaning of Jesus's parable of the Good Samaritan? Explain. Using few words.*

***

I wasn't prepared to provide an interpretation for Samson's weakness, Delilah's guile, Noah's drunkenness, and King David's filicide inside a study guide/ scarred with reamed lines. They resembled directional arrows, pointing to a lectern. I imagined hundreds of Bible study kids, stifled, stammering in front of the lectern. And no platitudinous opinion I offered was much different than theirs. It wasn't a happy dream. It was in fact much happier imagining a hundred hands awkwardly scribbled anything/ not special/ no one's answer particularly better than the others.

***

And I still see my lanky Bible study peers crestfallen/ verging spiritual ejaculations/ mirror imaging synopses illustrated inside the study manuals/ who were too young to realize they lived in sociological Sodom and Gomorrah's/ before the youth choir pews began filling with pregnant baby bellies/ on the verge of relating *Revelations* to the facts of life/ who didn't appreciate why *deliver us from sin and lead us not into temptation* hit close to home/ and why in the coming chapters of subsistence all the poverty cherubs and angels received wages sin, sensuality and labor divvied between work horses and show horses/ and Billy, Benny, the danky nameless kids, the irascible Harvey, his sisters, cousins and his flashy BFF, who couldn't stop screaming, *stop teasing me boy*, Cheryl Brewer, Debra Scott and the nameless muddy girl who put her hands in my pants/ all the Bible study kids caught up in its centrifuge —

***

— like several generations of the children of Ham/ who rode the yellow school buses/ who recognized each other (their mirror images: mirror imaging) when they reached Mrs. Austen's Bible study class/ at St. Paul Missionary Baptist —

— like novices on a mad carousel —

***

Since my bygone religiosity, sure, I lost my knack for fathoming chapter and verse. The heavy cadences. The labyrinthine verses. The rhetorical contradictions. But I surprised myself by locating an old, tattered *King James* in between the stacks, racks, the forgotten library books. I commenced, by blighted light (in a room with a blown bulb). I suckered myself. Between seven o'clock, ten o'clock, dreamtime, I played fast and loose with my Southern Baptist upbringing. I rummaged hopscotch, hastily, back, forth. I barely finished ten pages (near the beginning, sandwiched in the middle, nearer the end) ere (archaic words like 'ere' seeping into my drowse like the plop   plop   plop of a leaky drain
plop

plop)
I barely perused ten pages ere I heard crying, cackling, and laughter intermingled with screams from a nearby park/ an imaginary scene/

***
like a mad carousel

***

like a mad carousel —
screams; chuckles —
challenges; chastisements —
an automated merry-go-round crashing past regulations; past the systemic controls —
while profiles distantly remembered from Sunday school classes stood on the sides tut-tutting and shouting *slower*

slower

while a handful of unfamiliar adults in the foreground hysterically applauded
— *faster   faster*

faster
while all the kids I remembered at St. Paul Missionary
Baptist huddled and circled like astral bodies on a rickety mad mechanism

***

And following/ chapter and verse/ Psalms and Corinthians/ I woke up in
Encino (but in the dream the pronunciation sounded like *echo, echo, echo*
California)/ the horizon in California sparkled like a tourist photograph
(better than imagery in glossy reproductions)/ living in cohabitation with
Dolly and Joey —

***

In Encino/ in California/ partnered with stereotypically sunny names.

***

— living in surreal contentment vs. topsy-turvy malcontent/ with an Asian
beauty/ like a plastic doll. Her Anglicized name was Dolly. I disliked her
shrillness, her manners, her imagery: strikingly cliché: stereotypically lovely:
broken English. Hot/ *manga-* cartoonish/ big-breasted/ Dolly/ and mopey
Joey/ her son by a previous partner/ we three lived in a loft space/ the apt.
caught first light/ soot-heavy. There were times when the pollutants weighed
on us ignobly/ Dolly chuckled when I described the loft windows/ 'tainted'
glass suggested stained/ 'stained' suggested the glass marred beneath
Encino pollutants resembled colored church glass/ her laughter was hot and
cackling/ breaking plates/ cackling projecting my bad conscience.

***

Frightened to touch our Bibles. We waited to earmark them, when told. The
Book — back at home — sat silently rearranging the idolatry of my interior.

***

Occasionally as with descriptions of a lucid dream —
in which the dreamer realizes the material is unreal —
I pierced the veils/ Dolly was a stereotype/ dumbed-down/ cheesecake that
I criticized in books, plays and films. But primarily the narrative was self-
disgusted. I stayed with her because cohabitation provided a stable financial
relationship. I pitied the nine year old (or was he ten? Or eleven?) Every
sequence involving Dolly appeared vaguely pornographic. And reeked of a
movie shot behind closed doors. The dream like an uninvited crack in a door.

***

In those days there was no king;
    like a mad carousel —
every man did what was right in his own eyes.

***

I wanted to scream, *bitch*. Bathsheba. Delilah. Dolly resembled a
mechanistic neurosis, stuck in a specific place and hour, while Joey
pretended she was a better mother/ holding her bloodless hand/ because he
resembled a magical astronaut who time traveled his history of lost identities
precipitously instigated.

***

Familiarity bred contempt, while complacency abetted carnality. Self-
contempt/ in this particular case/ behind self-projections.

***

I flipped random pages/ shrill and mud-colored tainted light —

***

                    like an astronaut who shrank to nothingness inside
his space suit morning after morning until I accompanied him on a short

32

journey to an impoverished restaurant. I attempted to say beforehand the diner was *El Cheapo*. Kid pleaded. We go greasy spooning. I entertained him/ poor boy/ victim of his crackpot mother/ by catching the tainted light inside a cylinder glass/ because I wanted him to understand a bad dream was a madcap stitch of grey days, memories, lies, and prayers. And tainted light/ mugging the cylinder/ mythically as hot wax meanders inside a lava lamp/ represented *for we see now through a glass darkly/ but then we will see whole*.

***

Particular memories from my Southern Baptist childhood carry the mustiness of an old hymnbook. Particular memories possess essences hauntingly biblical — or the heaviness — or the mustiness of dust, death, solemnity, miserable shock.

Pray tell. I flipped random passages of a *King James*. Finding Voices. Incantations. Exhortations. Sublimity. Brutality. Cupidity. Pursuing memories — passages that ring a bell — and lacking another way to convey my impressions.

like a mad carousel

There is a palimpsest inside random recollections. This is the nature of memory's book. The crux is realizing that whether you have glanced at a tattered *King James*, or whether you have studied *King James* scrupulously — in refined detail — any Bible/ its thickness/ its archetypal significance/ is memory's book. Pray tell. You will discover/ rediscover/ uncover the good, the bad, the ugly. You'll probably land on passages that inspire, and passages that dismay. Passages that seem unforgivably crude. Passages that soar lovingly. Passages that vaguely disorientate. And not-so vaguely disgust. The crux remains/ is memory's book. And crucifies consciousness.

***

Even the ugliest passages from **Leviticus**/ buried in its secret cache/ *If a man commits adultery with another man's wife — with the wife of his neighbor — both the adulterer and the adulteress must be put to death*/ speak to an angst/ your misguided upbringing. And pride and vanity/ the stoning deaths/ the war plunder/ *As for the women, the children, the livestock and everything else in the city, you may take these as plunder for yourselves*/ measures your unresolved violence. Traps you inside its imagery. The feeling stays with you that all chapters lay on slanted foundations. There is nothing to playfully, thoughtlessly, or conveniently extract from the whole.

***

flipping back and forth until I woke up in Encino/ *Echo Echo Echo* California was lined with strip malls and congested traffic zones/ children's screams intermingled with carnival music/ and we couldn't tell whether the sounds were painful/ miserable/ desperately jubilant/ I finally took Dolly's child on a Sunday excursion down the streets and together we happen on a parkland oasis/ inside it a classic horse and carriage ride/ fifty cents a ride/ not like a royal suite/ left unpainted since the early seventies/ the color scale values industrial/ the kid and I watched this piece of creaky machinery/ alongside the threadbare trees and insignificant leaves turning a color no one visited a parkland oasis/ to bother sightseeing/ a thin handful of children atop ponies bobbing up/ bobbing down/ we stargazed rather than return to a household drowned beneath heavy/ tainted light/ and I squeezed his hand sympathizing with his stifled rage/ my stifled angst/

poor craftmanship on a shoddy carousel —

that mocked childhood expectations/ I imaged scores of children at St. Paul Baptist never/ daring to mistreat their Bibles/ who learned to mistreat their bodies/ sex/ violence/ flipping through its lowly majesty/ Samson and Delilah's tawdry knock offs/ until I woke up in *Encino Echo Echo*/ we knew we would remember this day and this hour for/ our allotted hours/ Joey refused to let himself enjoy a pony/ just a fifty cent ride/ let him enjoy himself/ let him sort through memories/ without benefit of beatitudes/ *if thine eye offend thee pluck it out*/ racing past delirium nearing sedentary dozing to/ ere I/ faster   faster

faster

The Shriveled Condom

— is a brethren to the worm. Get real. Get honest. *Get a post-prophylactic life!* When you see a tossed condom, what do you then see? When you see a wastrel rubber, lying near the roadside? Or underneath the bedside? When you see a spent condom discarded, oozing miserably? A spent condom leaks sexual afflatus — a degradation of sexual potency to its waste product effluvium, leakage, unborn babies, a swansong to the hearty Good American Boy appetites.

##

Don't gag. Don't file a complaint with city management/ waste disposal. Better yet. Don't look.

##

The balloon burst. The microwaved cake macro-degraded. The milk curdled. The imagery lies in decomposition. Looking at it is counterintuitive — scrutinizing a crushed, colorless, and uncamouflaged discarded condom stewing in its juices, seed and drivel is studying the uncategorizable. It's something sensitively mucous, plastic, elastic, mammalian. Its indefinability influences what else you will see. A lowliness wedged uncomfortably in between being and nothingness, the materials disassembling. It is the subject that you can't study without recollecting the poultice that you can't touch, the cavern that you hesitantly, sheepishly crawl inside, before acknowledging the creepiness that you can't shake. *Pepto-Bismol* may help.

##

Blink three times. A spent condom lies like a smashed thingamajig, the entrails spilling insectoid matter. A sliminess unearthly, unnatural. An inchworm slithered into midday foot traffic.

##

The spent rubber will never be usable again. Its shelf life — its physiological life span — or the length and longevity of it in a past time right now is barely thinkable.

The fresh-from-the-packet condom isn't much better. Its color palette is unappetizing. Its latex stickiness, lubricity, and pinkish color might make a half-decent primitive watercolor. A notable exception is slimy art in the manner of a dripping, oozing, and nauseating Dali masterpiece: *The Persistence of (Bad) Memories*.

##

Dali's slimy answer to Greco-Roman statuary.

##

A withered, wearied worm.

##

Christian Enzensberger's **Smut: An Anatomy of Dirt**, a rarified German literary classic (the English edition is a collector's item which with luck can be found in between a garishly pink and modernist cover) proclaims that the principle of cleanliness and godliness is a matter of the materials conforming to a particular epidermal size, shape, and schema; the unclean species conform to nobody's business. Enzensberger writes "Or the class itself confounds the general schema of the world … The case of the worm will always be remarkable. For a worm is not something below but something all around. In fact the worm also turns out to be limbless with ill-defined limits, still capable of living when cut up into pieces – as if its peculiar element dissolved anything resembling individuality …"

##

The Great Goddess Archetypal Earth Mother/ Sister and Lover reading the above leers and smiles making note that a male appendage is prototypical yet individuated (like a dog named Sam, Chuck, or Spot) while a rubber "confounds" while unindividuated. And unfeeling. Like a bug, a slug. Having a rubber "cut up into pieces" is consequently so much less of a tragedy.

##

While one wrinkled lowlife provides indispensable protection against social diseases, the other subaltern exudes indispensable richness into the soils. Touché.

##

The Great Goddess Archetypal Mother/ Sister and Lover says: Protect yourself. Protect the planet.

##

Its 'limbless ill-defined limits' wormed in your hands on the very night you lost your virginity. Something tricky happened. You couldn't pin it down, a sticky snakeskin, an uncategorizable cocoon disappeared up your sleeves. It slithered inside your palm, under the backside, back again, in and out and beneath the bed sheets. It returned — like a sea gift — and raveled into a double helix challenging you to unknot it, come on, come on, kid, do your best, this might be your best shot. "Losing it" couldn't mean failure in a New York minute? Couldn't it? Whew. Dumb luck retrieved a second condom. The Lady-in Waiting retrieved it from a compartment in her pocketbook. The denouncement was conveniently *Deux ex Machina*.

##

The Great Goddess Archetypal Mother/ Sister and Lover says the story feels contrived to justify male stupidity and dependence on feminine archetypes, female munificence, or guile. The subtext implies: Dysfunction is by hook, or crook a feminine responsibility.

##

The Great Goddess Archetypal Mother/ Sister and Lover advises: Grow up. *Touché*.

##

The condom/ the worm scoff at your inability to appreciate them — emblems of a responsible planet: each sanitizes an ecosystem. Alright, so on an intellectual level you have begun to see. And speaking of prejudices, errors, implicit bias, you may have been unjustified associating them at all. *Touché*.

##

A stain on the balustrade.

##

The Great Goddess Archetypal Mother/ Sister and Lover says: Let love rule. Love is trust. Cultivate a sense of obligation for all humankind. Cultivate a no-nonsense appreciation of social responsibility and sexual morality. Do not fear malfunction, and in a pinch try again. *Touché*.

##

Mistakes. You never proposed to Rochelle. You behaved cavalierly, and visited her with flowers, or gifts, or lively propositions so sporadically that while she always sympathized with "a gentle and sweet" soul (you?) she drifted to other lovers. Why didn't you seize the opportunity when you had her enthralled? And you knew you had her enthralled because she was the first girlfriend — the Alpha and Omega actually isn't shortlisted — regardless she was the most generous when she redressed the plight. It became so habitual that you didn't have to ask W*ill you help me put it on?* (It was actually a long while before you stopped asking.) The modulations in your voice drift through your mind: matter-of-fact, a bit somber, dopily confident, or wryly amused. *Will you help me put it on* is the kind of request which hinges on self-identity (fear of rejection) so resolutely that it can't sound like a clarion cry. Or insofar as it is a clarion cry it is also a plea for mercy. *Will you help me put it on?* is sweet, or sad, until it is pathetically echolalic. Rochelle was always receptive, magnanimous, skillful, nimble-fingered, relieving the possibility of fumbling before getting it on — a condom tip hanging limply half-uninflated. Wasn't she shamelessly, shamelessly practical-minded?

##

There was one particularly sweet lover who used to help you take it off. And the way she gently handled the flaccid post-coital phallus, the spittle-slick condom, beginning with gently unrolling the latex sheath layer, by layer, and roll after roll, with fingers no less willing to handle a bag of wet bread slices, the sensitivity of it melted something inside a core and deeply intimate place. Her sensitivity at "a touchy moment" made you rethink past attitudes, honest to God, why didn't you marry her? Without a stint, first, she touched it "the worm" — listen — then you heard a whisk in the air and felt her pitch the crumpled condom into the dark. The recesses in the outer dark. Clammier than the shelf dark. Clammier than the closet dark. It's out there (down there) beneath the bed somewhere, listen, listen. It smacked the bedside bureau. It hunkered near the nightstand. It burrowed inside the carpet folds. Slick. Slimy. Still drawing energy from its seminal juices, and detritus, distress or weathered damage. Worm!

Autumnal

Three complacent generals
burgeoning to dry dusty
tin soldiers. Tanks a far cry
from battle steel. No chance
of ready victories. They already
believe this. The clocks
on either side of their offices turning
backwards. A desk map describes
projects stalled last fall. Poppy
fleurs in the dank unwatered vases
foresee entropy beginning
to pack up the bags
shrinking sprightliest seeds autumnal.

The Room Light

Is killing a man
between the crosshairs
of his stealthy being. But he
will never accomplish
his cleansing and re-ordering
dusting the objects
in this dank room: a space ship

stuck in the clouds.
The light is too dim.
The screen leaves smoke trails.
The blasted bulb ungrips
a heaven of penumbras
rocketing past the eons
like the gradual leavening
of his healthy pulse: his acuity: each
strengthless half-past seven towards evening.

Downtown Lounge

Evening descends like svelte jet-black hair

unbundled. And beneath the Empyrean stairs

starshine stiletto heels/ a proscenium

blazoning disco lights instead of clothes;

poptart lipstick/ a thin, cherry red design/

three bright gold teeth smiling, the grossest devil-may-care

And They Say

A young man speaks…

'heard there was a legend
nearby. Damn. I see a tree.
                           a Spanish Oak
Neither death, nor the sun …
Neither death, nor the sun …
Nature's Gogoltha. Or a green Ragnarök.
A church letting out. A family
vanishing into the shadeless block.
I kind of detest the blaze of Southern legends
hm, less pure than simple lies.
It may be gossip's swiftest
avenue to retooling its alibi
for cruelty …

   legend has it the man
was lynched, noosed, his flesh charred
unrecognizably as afterbirth,
his clothes tossed to the rags
of history, an oil-soaked, human torch.
His body just a clock
broken by drunken sailors,
slammed against a brick wall, loosening
the memory of pain's instruments un-
                           charted.

He was twisted beneath a limb
preserved in a square on *blank* street,
the oak still living, serpentine, Gothic,
longer than any accusatory finger.
The family approaches. To read a plaque,
I guess. Naw. The garden fence is only
to protect the tree, maybe,
from pests, locusts, and *blank* odd threats.

The victim lay blinded first.
He was a soldier … his heirs, his relatives …
say this, say that … Or who says much
beside the steady erosion of tic, tock.
Trace his body in civic sands.
Trace a memorial in the public dust.
This is a Maypole Sunday. Adults
matter less than esplanade children,
kids still matter more than strangers.

Not oak not ivy could make the tale
charming. Or pretend history *isn't*
a playground rumor. I shouldn't say that
anyhow. No matter the last surviving witness
stands like a testimony which faintly
incriminates: like silences after a death.
Still was a ceremonial killing, I guess.
'spect the dead inhale. Exhale. Like memory's breath.
Pretend the oak tree called for a funeral hush.
Pretend happenstance may honor it

like a storm which turns away from ghost houses,
And they say …
— rumor, legend, gossip is a contour
A profile in sidewalk chalk, a bag of bone.
None of the skeletal anatomy filled in
nor veins. Children crayon inside it colorfully.
I heard about a fable woman, conjurer,
slave, though she was real, neither, both,
— I still know she was *black*, no rites
of the festooned macabre changed that.
Human scarifications. Her lips sewn shut.
Probably talked too much. They said.

Hm. Guess she was *alive*. Her nasty fibs
punished. Now the story's a retired flag
folded up, till it flaps in the breeze
Occasionally it snaps like a pocketbook
        My tongue clucks like a pocketbook.
My life beneath the limb of a story
playing a stranger's
        My life playing a respectful Sunday stroller's
part in a dumbstruck village
is over. The present begs the way to live

        together here.

November Beginnings

And after the many hours
I spent/ I whiled/ crisply sodden
self-involuted as a spider
the air ungripped …
kitchen sigher room glider
room glider
kitchen sigher
and the heat, the cold, the dross is *what* a riddle.

***

nomenclature
would not spare me
the nights and days
breaths lacquered
in puffy frostiness
cursing was a coverlet

***

My body is not
your body and if it isn't
mine either then the days
November/ would be well-spent
recuperating before/ after conflicts.

***

Behaving like a ship
-tossed sailor
topsy-turvy unhinged
I steered the
coldest domesticated metal
-lic objects in the room
— clutched for the sake of shock.

***

I lost and found/ lost
the pulse in the
blood clenching
inundated veins
to cornstalk tips …
blood ran riot —
ruthless in the grip of it.

***

From the window
glass — frequent
backwards glances — I watched
rain nurturing
shimmering places
crystal palaces/ snow people

sinisterly sanguine
    and mama, mama, oh
        and the irrepressible mother of forgetfulness

***

Three nights straight
I shaved. Three nights straight
I slid the blades up and
across stubbled skin
the threatening edge bewildering
all beggars at the gate
maladroitly mismanaging
Gillette steel
razors
on the cheap/ no lather/
to make myself
burn …

Fragmented by Frenetic Erasure

]
]

The hospital mummy
In whitey whites awaits
Time's green relief

]

And time-in-a-bottle. Victim of an elusively

          impatient
]
]

                           Non-committal
    Post-surgical system

]
… naked salves whitening beneath the sunlit awning

]

… his stained salves, nitpicked bandages,
purple his lower extremities; the growth

the steady seepage, *damn spot*

]

is as insoluble as a marker inserted inside a diseased fish

]

— bloodier than home ghosts. A sleek
green pulsing sheen. The absinthe coming.
… snaps, finger-clicking,
cracks his rock-solid mouth

]
]

like Jesus's cold vault

]

O woman at Gethsemane

]

O princess at the courtyard tables

]

clucks his tongue, *bitch   bring me a —*

]

bring me special attentions
        bring me sweet libations

]
]

his hand's five-fingered concertina
and arachnid crawl,
pulls the tablecloth,
and timpani drums, *bring me an absinthe coming!*

]

— he points, as he sees the green bottle floating
                heels clattering
        like pebbles spraying
                  a swirl of broken stones
              instead of rain —
"pardon me" he says, points, begrudging himself his gross apparition.

]

beneath the café awning
    a streak of motion sashays, as
        a woman hands a man
        in a bind the flask's green-hued waters,
lightly, but brusque, she draws a bill; coins, bills,

blood, bottleneck; silvery blurry heaps —

green crowns the tray
and tops the steeple like St. Patrick's Day carnage.

]
]

The bottle is indecipherably translatable. Greenness is like
                              dayness
and spectacle plight.

Green. Color of four-leaf clover.
Bottle green. He remembers fallen drunks.
Color of St. Patrick's Day parades, bountiful
Bacchanalia. Confusion, chaos, crowds of feverish inebriates,
lining stained streets, lostness.

]

Blood breaking through —
restitching the unstitching
His hospital dress is —
suit no silver lining
Color of broken noses.

]

His tongue is a prelate,
servicing water and blood,
steadies himself, waits,
dreads the stone
And turns to
the sun, like a stone

a blazoning stone. His teeth manifest.

— manifesting like rough
craggy spikes in low pools.

]

Tomb light

— bursts through revealing
rows of sunken teeth, the grit that's
trashily luminous. Spirits in stained
robes, lightly stained green,
lightly stained scarlet.
Ghostly evanescent saints.
Briefly radiant angels.

Pantoums for James Meredith

James Meredith Goes to School at the University of Mississippi. 1962

The campus buzzed like cheesecake-era sexual innuendo.
Shocking pale nudes in *Studio Art* were *still* white.
A fetish in freshmen sociology? Black beyond sightless.
An abyss spellbinds an archeologist. Ole' Miss cheerleaders blush.

Shocking Manet nudes in *Art History* were still *all* white.
We cheered Mississippi football heroes. But joshed the second stringers.
An ignoble statuette fascinates *artistes*. Makes a blind man blush.
We still cursed. And drank until in a stupor we mooned the sun.

We cheered football heroes. But teased the second stringers.
We rolled a fetish between sore thumb and forefinger. Meredith?
We cursed. We drank until in a stupor we mooned the sun.
We ran naked in rings naming him under ungodly pretenses.

We rolled a fetish in between sore thumbs and fingers. Him?
The savage doll stained the last days fast coming.
We ran in rings naked summoning him under ungodly pretenses.
Then something like anger sucked the heat from our fingers.

The blackness resembling *blankness* stained the last days fast coming
crowding moon-soaked lawns. The grass still wet. We lay.
But something like anger sucked heat from our fingers.
The moonlight screened movies. Silent lessons. *Birth of a Nation*

crowded moon-soaked lawns. The grass still wet. We lay
witnessing scenes perversely prideful. But sweet.
The moonlight screened movies. There was *Birth of a Nation*
abbreviated to a glory cry. Next movie. Entitled *horseplay*,

pairing us with women perversely ample. But sweet.
We dreamed of the incoming class's beauty pageant bombshells
abbreviated to a glory cry. Sigh. It culminated in horseplay
starring Mansfield rippling in the grass. We must be men.

We dreamed hopelessly of beauty pageant bombshells.
Miss Mississippi 1962 soaks her nails. Gawks. Dreams
she's Mansfield rippling in the grass. We must be restored to men
protecting innocence already strained from blindness. Blankness. Sin.

The campus buzzed like cheesecake-era sexual innuendo.
Miss Mississippi 1962 soaks her nails. Gawks. *He's coming.*
A fetish in freshmen sociology? Black beyond sightless.
Class of '62 erupts, in between blindness. Terror. Or sin.

***

The following day

Banners waft on a breezy afternoon.
Huh? Is a football hero coming?
Signs stuck planted on a fiery lawn
brazenly beleaguer his freshman welcoming.

Huh? Is Jesus Christ Himself soon coming?
Somebody hauls a Cross from a truck,
then sparks it blazoning unwelcoming.
Nigger. Nigger go home.

Somebody hauls an old rugged sacrificial
Cross from an idle pick-up truck.
Nigger, Nigger please go home.
Somebody mutters why should a field coon

Cross the line near the pick-up truck.
Epithets coagulate bloodier than sunsets.
Somebody mutters Mother Mary, Oh, Sweet Mary
Madonna. Has the wretched revelation been coming?

Epithets coagulate a color of sunset crimson.
Banners meanwhile waft on a breezy afternoon
rehabilitating rebel insignia. Soon coming.
Violence ignites on a fiery lawn.

How to Live with Racism, In Times Like These

... and so ...?

Become used to the feeling
at all times, that the flesh,
flagellated, feverish puffiness
in particular the poignant places
where the vertebrae curves
is melting, melting, to *angst* gone to crap.

Study the stool/ such daily craps
like a horoscope: synchronized to feelings
how functional systems midway curve
until past internalized bile mulches flesh
pours into the heartfelt places
susceptible to psychosomatic illness (puffiness)

Practice using herbs and lotions/ puffiness
calcifies the skin's breath/ asthma is crap
still psychically undigested. Benign places
where you suffer sudden stress feeling
an atavistic stiffness hammer flesh
to an ancient bone. And a bad back curves.

Negative socialization stymies sleep, curves
sally to cripwalk, toothsomeness to puffiness
self-enfolding lumps of riddled flesh
bulk beneath shy lids/ sleep's a crap
-shoot in a puzzled welter/ feelings
stiffen like chess pawns in the wrong places.

Acknowledge the health burdens angst places
in between dolor and the daily curves/
Murphy's law/ throwing sobriety to feeling
— if judgement intervenes — hives, cancer, puffiness,
the apocalypse's four horsemen coming crap
all over a calm facade. Death is inherent in the flesh.

And death's mode in bad times is bruised flesh
softening slowly in the wrong places
listless fatigue leaves shit, crust, crap
putrefying the toilet rim/ meals skipped/ curve
balls self-implode memory/ socks sacrificed/ puffiness
is generic putty: enthusiasm low: no feeling.

———————————

cut the crap   feed the flesh   avoid black outs

— because honestly speaking they're sudden relief —

*Taking a breather allows/ one-shot self-analysis
less urgent care than homing in on memory lapses:*

finish tasks/ scrub the tub

walk the dog/ tip the jar   round the curves

*round the curves
struggle with memory against forgetting to see: eye strain: a
            feeling of puffiness in places*

beware/ struggle with memory against forgetting

                              to flush.

And that Same Old Song and Savage Splendor

Erasure poem using the first chapter of
Truman Capote's Other Voices, Other Rooms

Now a traveler must make his way ...
Noon City — best means he can. No buses or trains.
Occasionally catch a ride/ rough trip/
    these washboard roads
                    loosen up;
hitchhikers always find the going bad.

        lonesome country ...

... swamplike hollows/
lilies the size of a man's head;
luminous green logs like drowned corpses;
movement is a sorry-looking wing-stiffened bird
circling over the black deserted
pinewoods.

... over the hinterlands into Noon City —
from the North ... South ... much the same.
Desolate swamp along routes unbroken
except for the signs advertising 5¢
Cigars. And wooden bridges named for long-gone

           Indian tribes

              rumbling like thunder.

Herds of hogs/
cows roam at will/
A farm family pauses from work ...
waves as an auto whizzes
            by. They'll watch till
It disappears in red dust. A Ford.

Pick-up type. Its interior smells
of sun-warmed leather. A broken speedometer
registered petrified twenty; crushed insects
blurred a windshield shattered in a bursting
-star pattern. A toy skull ornaments the gear shift.

 — wheels over the rising, dipping
highways — child scrunched chin-cupped —
beneath January rain
and naked tree limbs,
bump-bumping like a sack
of shriveled tangerines.

       Noon City …

Puzzlements. A pair of spectacles with green, cracked lenses.
Days melt. Everything something it isn't.
A splinter from the Sprite's evil mirror.
Grown-up legends. Or frightened, guilty first letters.
A honeymoon suitcase dragged down from an attic.

Clumps
Of Negro cabins. Clapboard church
with three Holy panes. Japonica trees with blackgreen polished
                                leaves.

       Not much to look at …

One street.
A *General Merchandise.* A
combination barbershop-beauty
parlor run by the one-armed man.
A curious indefinable *RV Lacey's* establishment
where a Texaco gas pump stands. Buildings
ramshackle. Haphazard overnight carpentry.

The jail hasn't housed
   a white criminal in four years
 — seldom a prisoner of any kind *albeit*
it is said three exquisite sisters
   … raped here by the fiendish
Yankee bandit who wore a cloak stained
scarlet blood of Southern womanhood;
it is a tale of Gothic splendor.

  lonesome country's crush of lichen, legacy, beatings,
blue bloods and black blood splendor …
… contradictions arise in celebration, in consternation …
Death and decay revisited, in sweet evocation, undead …

Stranger in a Legal Land

Three men have lassoed one man in an utterly strange
— such a strange — still an intractable
embrace. One man's pupils shimmer darkly as three
triangulated flashlights intersecting
piercing his immobilized flesh
as though he has been fitted three apparitional
faces; a Triptych of rumor and speculations'
swaddling clothes enveloping coyly
uncoiling hydras of indeterminate intentions.
The shadowing of such inarticulate affairs is gray.
The status of such indeterminate plans is *stand down*.
The accused stands mid-center like a smudgy emblem.
Crapola of the realm; chump change; a trashy penny.
He stands mid-center like a representation of the prodigal son
in Rome; he has wandered from the stone kingdoms;
far fields; the rocky provinces; the hinterlands;
the counties of lawless pursuits; heavy breathing; loose
-lipped legends of lapidary prizes; ancestral reprisals.
Conflicting stories, strung around himself like primitive beads.
Three men impromptu critique one man's dress.
Backwardness inherent in his knobby-gnarly haberdashery.
His livid scarifications; his colorfully antique tattoos
portraying finely stitched pictograms — following
the first blinks — that sidle his ghastly limbs
unrepentantly illustrating somebody's dubious prospects.
The lack of modesty behind his anachronisms
insulting any portraitist's idealized stove top hat.
And then the compass point fire burgeons
fork-tongued licks winding up, up the loose shirt sleeves.
Conflicting tales worn around his neck like beads.

A Southern Plantation Memory

A Flashback.
Rain: rendering the historic mansions of the plantation
South so aptly weather-winnowed/
storm-soaked and cowl drenched/
storm gust-curtained. The facades
no longer staring
— for a few empty hours —
like eyeless sockets. Not
after the watery runnels
and richly inclement clouds
pull my shades

down. And memory is less,
less reliable at the end of the road.
The town and country is a surreptitious forecast.
The storied greenery is blinding blanketed oblivion.
The Southern old order is rinse/ wash/ and drizzle.
The *ancien régime* is out of business a while.
It's like that. Regardless.

Rain slashing the windshields
crashing into the headlights
like the past breaking
into siren-songs
and robbing Peter to pay Paul.
Rain muddying the stop signs.
Rain burying the legacies unearthly
hurling the spirits of the slave
-dead deeper into their whitewashed anonymity.
Rain shadowing the columns.
Rain pummeling the graves.
It's like that. Total
pastoral magic. Or
else rain.

The Man Staring into the Partial Dark: A Ghazal

… coughing into late hours … a wall is blank oblivion
blanker than the night passes … no sheath is blank oblivion.

The partial dark is a Rembrandt motif on a half shell
crimped several shades short, less absolute than *frank* oblivion.

He brushes the dusty bits from his body: rolls: catches his death: curses:
smoldering while his fragmentary dark tanks oblivion.

His best sleep is hunchbacked, much less when some feverish effluvium
stains the sheets; his body basking in sweat that stank oblivion.

He hears chimerical giggling splitting hairs on his forehead —
But he wishes the dark was whole rather than memory's Manx oblivion.

In the fifth grade, a brunette with the strangest Greek name
told him his name was English derivative, before the archaic twaddle ranked
oblivion.

His bashful Greek brunette promised to leave his secret in drawers: like
coy love notes. *Darryl. Darling, lover.* Like letters lost in nostalgic oblivion.

His name derived from Old English baby talk, and *de facto* any nocturnal
voices calling him whether screeching *Go to hell and back* still seductively hedged
against oblivion.

And let the love names echo, selfsame cooing sibilants, *dearling, de Airelle, Darryl,*
sighs to nursing babies, bodies in sickness, health, and the whole dark that thanks
oblivion.

Sunlight Erasing Lines, Margins on a Pencil Drawing

   to look, to see, behold,
strew, spread, revise,
opening one's eyes,
underlining with a red/ yellow/ black marker
rubbing smooth any particular sort, kind, type,
every line is a pencil draft
to let sunlight crush, crunch, reassessing
the parts, or points that lead
Outside, beyond an enclosure,
any barrier, the world outside civilization,
(breaking it down inclusively, not
forgetting prison, nor the army) any
short piece of writing, short scrimmage of
sketch, in pencil, ink or crayon, to strip,
to tie ruled lines down with a cord,
set in alignment, misalignment,
making something coming to nothing much,
stinging *alas* like sea salt
self-destructive black bars, sun streaks, shapes, shadow
hordes retracing ordinary work.

A Spiritual Emanation/ Ejaculation

throw ash on an unburied bone
tie a cup on a string to summer green apple trees
Pick it up   voices revealed
pseudo-electrical surges   like a lightning bolt discharged
and a nonentity-in-the-wire crackles:
throw ash on an unburied bone
hang up/   the fractured bone is healed

Easy Street. Or, The Year of Getting a Driver's License and Exciting Eldritch Regions of Consciousness

Taking a cue from the sweet effluvium or (so-called) sickle moon, maybe "the dead of night" is no valley of bones, just a figure of speech, the young kid itches to take the family car under screaming streetlamps on a spin; his soul escapes the house like air whizzing from an unknotted balloon, or a space craft hovering in pursuit of the facts which can be drawn from a colorful expression. Last year, surrounded by school buses like enemies, he thought. *The dead of night is a cradle of ghostly life.*

Blobs haunt errant estates. Stick against the tar-black pits. Radiance bubbles out of sinkholes. Crawling Etruscan Neon. Neon slurps uptown like an oozing movie monster. Time supersedes timeliness, and a wisp of air blows out of the funereal house, an estate sick and tired of disciplining a voyager of vaguer purposes than a philosopher looking at his own imminent death on a watch without a second hand. Emptiness? Eleven o'clock — ergo — is elastic. E. Street bridges 'beyond good and evil' at the crack of the devil.

Street sepulchral is a cradle of ghostly life.

This is the year of getting even-steven. The street is a flash of a black coat — estranged undertaker servicing an urban underground. The street may keep statistics on the many thousands gone. Its denizens can't in turn detail its distinct characteristics. The length and breadth of *the street* is just a generalization, like birth, childhood, adolescence and first love. Hence the kid tends to assume the right to hang out anywhere. Erstwhile curfew hours: conceptually as problematic as the hours, minutes, seconds left to deconstruct whether his license plate is a ticket into a movie theater called society owes me a fun time at equitable cost. Kid ponders whether Easy St. beneath the new moon is Horus' sarcophagus. Eleven o'clock eastern standard time. His cherubic face albeit precludes XXX clubs.

Street sepulchral is a cradle of ghostly life.

The Golgotha of his coming-of-age is *Avangelo's* pool hall, *Open at Ten*. Kid never too discouraged to hope. And peek. Sedan steers feelings there must be somewhere worth going when evening promulgates semaphores, at a second thought. An obstructed stop sign reads *Easy St. 666. No restrictions here.* He considers lying to his parents on a week-end, lying so that he can have thirty more minutes, forty five, at most another hour to drive the sedan. Kid parks near the pool hall — steers his shadow — catches a glimpse interior, poor kid, sees laughing, slightly lewd men and adult woman in an expressionistic thicket, and hears caws, like bird caws in the colorful rainforest distances. A pool stick on a billiard table wets his guilt. Exoticism exfoliates eroticism. Entails Egyptian Enigmas. Etruscan signage emanates *Establishment rules. Environmental hazards. Don't Drink and Drive. No Resurrections here*

Nature Proem

Looking at the vacuum cleaner,
I don't think about an operational
God: heavens no. But I may think about energy
the bizarre temporality of the objects
containing it. There is a street sweeper
outside distressing the neighborhood
with its chewing gnawing noisiness
and staring into its tumultuous
crescendo would probably be more like the abyss.
The vast tanklike supra-robot threatens
to put an end to this small and green
   planetary life
        an end to the pathetically shriveled
     skin and bone crushed beneath terrible metallurgy.
Death to the human race —
           Death to the human race!
Our dishonorable enterprise sucked up like slop.
The vacuum cleaner merely mocks my unplugged lethargy.

Days of Protest

We will smash the world
Wildly
We will thunder ...

Roses and dreams
Debased by poets
Will unfurl ...
— The 150 000 000, Mayakovsky

We will not disappear
like her birth name
like his dead letters
buried inside a sheaf
after a flash rain ...

We will not disappear.

***

Death yawns stately.
Death conjoins us.
— whether we make music
noise, love, or bourgeoisie war.
Free assembly and funeral
rites, these days, symbiotic, interchangeable.

Siren sounds. We will not disappear

***

we proceed like marionettes
carried along on one string
crowds of selfsame mouths
our tongues chant *now* in unison
the pitch like a cracked accordion
then canticle is cant
and cry.

and the dead also
They will not disappear.

***

Death conjoins us. The streets
indigenously compel us
whether we lay down
and recharge
screaming at planned events
protest marches
and vigils
have become
intermarried, like a sexual transgression

Death conjoins us

***

Death pulls back the curtain.
Public war,
like private mourning,
pulls back the curtain.
An old law is a heavy sigh.
Its retellings, latchkey shibboleth   *blood nurses grief,*
                    grief nurses war,

and what else is changed to soldiers and mourners?

***

We wear hoodies and chains
— hoodies, sneakers, jerseys, chains;
lining the streets carrying placards,
banners
and loudspeakers
amplifying *Trayvon   Breonna*
                  EricGarnerFreddieGreyPhilandoCastle
  like aggravated parlor ghosts
And sound systems reify the abstractions:
let the crowds inspire regardless
belief in eternal succession …

***

— then we seize the streets.

then we seize the streets at noon and night
but dispassionately challenge
standard badges of the numinous state;
officers in bright-dark svelte glasses breaking
past the front lines berate us.

The blue lines aggress.

        — but we seize the streets at night

***

We amplify. We reify.

    — we amplify using cost efficient
instruments of bulbs, amps, wattage;
crackle and hum breaks daylight monotony
then we seize the streets at noon and night
like visionary candlewicks afloat on
sea and surge. *But the sea will never*

        swallow the candles: burning brightly!

***

And amplify. And reify
flesh of my physical atrophy
death's indigenous people
shortchanged before destruction …
who will not disappear
like her birth name
like his dead letters
after a flash rain …

Contemplating Homelessness

A man thinking over what he will do
the day before he has to leave his house

tonight, and where to go, where to sleep

These same questions could be tendered to the stars
under the assumption philosophy warrants derision.
Or maybe not. Give me then the stars' dumb luck
in preference to the pointless blank
gaze of other systems: money that can't sweat
skip, run, jump, although it speaks
while pennilessness is rough, tanned, and muscular.
Poverty is pretty *louche*, in fact, and voiceless.
A final undeposited check may be a grand comedian.
Or maybe the awkward matter
is simply related to objects in transition —
things which can be put inside safe storage
things which can be easily disposed, junked, or sublimated
and objects consigned to an accumulated oblivion.
There is a place for mementos in limbo
like a purgatory for the silently depressed
facing streetwise catastrophe with too little
left to value against the cost of breaking even.

Thinking over friends, fear and laughter

Many years ago in a strangled past
which like every past or future under circumstances
when the stars have no other set intentions
and fate resembles vectors scribble-scratched
in a past which resembled *long, long ago*
far-far away — given the layers of past tenses proverbial —
I knew a grey man who owned properties and another

who managed the rentals. They kept long hours
unusually long hours in each other's company
for businessmen weathered by strife and commerce,
I suppose. I couldn't understand
their persistent laments. I was so impressed
simply because they related less
like an old guy speaking to his on-the-job
carpentry-skilled underling than friends, well,
yes, pals. Did that mean masterminds of helplessness?
     Did that mean understanding the laws of threat?
Did that mean robber barons upping rents?

I hung out drinking beer and coke
(between friends they never charged a cent) when
the sudden pall of business called. The regular
guy whispered. Knitted his brows;
the old man's blue eyes deepened. I remember
laughter, then the shadows, *contracts, law, leases.*

The mold

My address.
It's unimportant.
The eviction notice read: *Mold remediation at —*
It wasn't the most elegant apartment.
Nothing overstated. Including the rot.
The space was simpler than a threadbare capsule.
The front yard welcomed weeds. And hosted rocks.
Three rooms. And between them less to comment
on than the sum of domestic bric-a-brac
minus visible interstices. The old-timey furnace
flared too brightly. And the gas
ensconced me in welcomed heat midwinter
intermingled with drifts too pungent;
besides which the furnace rods clunked;

I stared into the clunky threat
feeling happier with all of it
than any happiness sustained in transit.
The mold must have arrived in secret
the way thieves, ghouls, or spies infiltrate

countries of the living who stubbornly imagine
themselves counting beads on an abacus
of coming days
whether the future is spent in a car
spent in a poverty trap
spent on a thread.

And where and how to sleep

Like a child's Crayola masterpiece
simplified to the point of colorful abstraction
any query presented literally: *where to go,*
where to spend the days and nights;
should I stay in a homeless shelter or my car
parked behind the monster trucks at Walmart?
can be reconfigured metaphysically
and the metaphorical offered to the stars
again: say sleepy-headedly *twinkle, twinkle,*
starlight, star bright, hoping
ruses in rhyme connect the dots.

The interstices between the starry pinnacles
may chart the image of a homeless man
sort of an exhausted yogi
proud how much self-knowledge he attains
testing the smallest spaces he can live inside.
Tonight then I'll drive until I find
shame inside a proper roach motel: humility, too,
between sleeplessness and first dawn light.

Acknowledgments

An early version of "And They Say" originally appeared in *Matter Monthly*

"God and Death" originally appeared in *Swimming with Elephants*

"Psalm Sequence" originally appeared in its entirety in *Blood Tree Literature*

"Nature Proem" was originally published in *Turtle Island Quarterly*

"Contemplating Homelessness" was commissioned by Creative Santa Fe for the presentation "Housing the Future 2.0" in 2019.

In "And that Same Old Song and Savage Splendor," I took artistic liberties creating line breaks, changing punctuation, adding "and" "the" and "albeit," and shifting tenses. Otherwise everything is from the mother text and appears in the exact order it appears in the mother text EXCEPT for the concluding four-line stanza, which is mine. You can check out Truman Capote's *Other Voices, Other Rooms* to see exactly what I have done.

About the Author

Darryl Lorenzo Wellington is the 2021-23 Poet Laureate of Santa Fe, New Mexico. An uprooted Southerner who is now a New Mexican, he has been a professional journalist for the over 20 years. His articles, fiction and poetry appear in *The Nation*, *The Atlantic*, *Dissent*, *The Washington Post*, *Boston Review*, *Yemassee*, *Drum Voices*, *Matter Monthly*, *The Pedestal Magazine*, *ABZ*, *Santa Fe Literary Review*, *Radius*, *Blood Tree Literature*, *Turtle Island Quarterly*, *Yellow Medicine Review*, and other places. His writing is anthologized in *MFA vs. NYC* (FSG, 2014) and *Santa Fe Noir* (Akashic Books, 2020). He is also a performance artist. His previous chapbook, *Life's Prisoners*, received the 2017 Turtle Island Poetry Award. *Psalms at the Present Time* is his first full-length collection.

CPSIA information can be obtained
at www.ICGtesting.com
Printed in the USA
FSHW021630281021

9 781945 824500

We will not disappear
like her birth name
like his dead letters
buried inside a sheaf
after a flash rain…

We will not disappear.

***

Death yawns stately.
Death conjoins us.
— whether we make music
noise, love, or bourgeoisie war.
Free assembly and funeral
rites, these days, symbiotic,
interchangeable.

Siren sounds. We will not disappear

***

we proceed like marionettes
carried along on one string
crowds of selfsame mouths
our tongues chant now in unison
the pitch like a cracked accordion
then canticle is cant
and cry.

—*from "Days of Protest"*

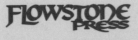

FLOWSTONE
PRESS

cover art by Marya Kirby

Psalms at the Present Time displays many tools at Darryl Wellington's command, including long, lyrical, and mesmerizing sentences, verbs that skip, leap, and scamper, and short, sharp phrases that land like percussion before lingering in the brain. Also part of his plentiful repertoire: thumbnail portraits of people, places, and things, the touch and tang of memories, and high-impact reflections rendered with a deft hand.

—Jabari Asim, Author of *We Can't Breathe*
and *Stop and Frisk: American Poems*

On and beyond the horizon, Wellington's excursions into our body politic, psyche, purpose, and existence are multilayered and multifaceted. Content and craft are given equal time and focus. There is a nuanced reacquaintance with poetry's significance in *Psalms at the Present Time*. This poet chooses sturdy ethos and empowering authenticity. It is a worthwhile expedition.

—Uche Nduka, Author of *Facing You*
and *Living in Public*

Darryl Lorenzo Wellington is the 2021-23 [P]
Laureate of Santa Fe, New Mexico. An upro[d]
Southerner who is now a New Mexican, he has be[en]
professional journalist for over 20 years, with arti[cles]
fiction and poetry in *The Nation*, *The Atlantic*, *B[...]
Review*, *The Washington Post*, and many other pl[...]

POETRY
$20

ISBN 978-1-945824-50-[...]
9000[...]
9 781945 824500